Forming a Successful Business Partnership

The 9 Things You MUST Consider When Starting a Small Business with a Partner and Creating a Business Partnership Agreement

by Jacklyn Saunders

Table of Contents

Introduction 1

Chapter 1: Selecting the Right Type of Business Partnership 7

Chapter 2: Deciding Between an Open or Closed Company 13

Chapter 3: Aligning Visions and Goals 17

Chapter 4: Defining Roles and Responsibilities 21

Chapter 5: Establishing How to Split Expenses and Profits 27

Chapter 6: Protecting Yourself When Banking with a Partner 31

Chapter 7: Signing Your Legal Signature 35

Chapter 8: Partnership Agreements to Put in Writing 39

Chapter 9: Dissolving the Partnership 43

Conclusion 47

Introduction

Starting a company takes time, dedication, and perseverance. More often than not, new business owners underestimate their own workload, especially in terms of what it takes just to get their company up and running. It's easy to burn through time and money without even realizing it, all of which is happening when the stakes are high and you're under pressure as you try to ensure the company's success.

Being an entrepreneur requires taking risks, as I'm sure you were aware when you signed up. And in this critical infant stage of your business, you know that if it doesn't work out, you may never recover from the loss of resources and self-esteem. This scenario is stressful and frustrating enough. Add a partner's expectations and differences of opinion, and it can have *disastrous* results. Now consider if that partner is a close friend or even a spouse.

Don't get me wrong, I'm certainly not suggesting that you should go it alone. Having a business partner can be incredibly advantageous, since that means you're sharing risk, responsibility, and financial investments. Considering these types of assets, having a partner may even be the difference between being able to start a company vs. falling short of having the resources you'd need to even begin. However, with that said, there are certain aspects of the partnership arrangement that you need to think about, talk about with your partner, and formalize in writing - yes, even if they're your spouse.

This book will lead you through the 9 specific components of business partnership that – for the sake of your company, your own personal finances, and your peace of mind – ***must*** be formalized in writing. It doesn't matter how well you (think you) know the person you are considering going into business with. The items covered in this book are absolutely crucial to the successful start and end of a partnership, and may well be just what helps protect the relationship you had together before starting the business.

If you are considering starting a business with a partner, or if you are already in the process of doing so, then this book is a must-read!

© Copyright 2015 by Miafn LLC - All rights reserved.

This document is geared towards providing reliable information in regards to the topic and issue covered. The publication is sold with the idea that the publisher is not required to render accounting, officially permitted, or otherwise, qualified services. If advice is necessary, legal or professional, a practiced individual in the profession should be ordered.

- From a Declaration of Principles which was accepted and approved equally by a Committee of the American Bar Association and a Committee of Publishers and Associations.

In no way is it legal to reproduce, duplicate, or transmit any part of this document in either electronic means or in printed format. Recording of this publication is strictly prohibited and any storage of this document is not allowed unless with written permission from the publisher. All rights reserved.

The information provided herein is stated to be truthful and consistent, in that any liability, in terms of inattention or otherwise, by any usage or abuse of any policies, processes, or directions contained within is solely and completely the responsibility of the recipient reader. Under no circumstances will any legal responsibility or blame be held against the publisher for any reparation, damages, or monetary loss due to the information herein, either directly or indirectly.

Respective authors own all copyrights not held by the publisher.

The information herein is offered for informational purposes solely, and is universal as so. The presentation of the information is without contract or any type of guarantee assurance.

The trademarks that are used are without any consent, and the publication of the trademark is without permission or backing by the trademark owner. All trademarks and brands within this book are for clarifying purposes only and are the owned by the owners themselves, not affiliated with this document.

Chapter 1: Selecting the Right Type of Business Partnership

If you are reading this book then you have put thought into the business you wish to start. You may have already done your market analysis and business plan. We will not go into those discussions here. Instead, this chapter looks at the different business structures. Since each business is different, you should consult a lawyer and an accountant to decide the best structure for you. This chapter will offer you an overview of the different possibilities to discuss with those professionals.

Sole Proprietorship: This entity is a pass through business structure. This designation is for one person who passes profits and losses onto a personal tax form. If you offer services without being an employee or owning a company, then you are a *sole proprietor*. A Sole Proprietorship does not offer protection from personal losses. Government offices use this designation to give licenses. It is included here to help you question your motives in bringing on a partner. Consider carefully if you need a partner for the business you will start. The only reason to bring a partner on board is if he has finances or contacts needed to move the business forward. If not, you might use employees to fill the role the partner may take in the business. By using employees, you still maintain control of the creative vision of the company.

General Partnership: A General Partnership happens as soon as you agree to work together on a business. This can be as simple as shaking hands with a friend over dinner on a creative idea. Next thing you know, you are working on the business every night after work. This is an easy designation to have, much like a Sole Proprietorship. If you work together then the business exists, no extra paperwork needed. The important thing to consider with this business type is that all profits and losses are shared equally. Not only do you share those, you share all liabilities, too. If your partner does something wrong and is sued, you are also liable for all expenses. Since this entity starts to exist with a handshake, consider carefully before verbally agreeing to anything. Try to have everything in writing instead. Also, consider a more formal structure for your business to limit your personal responsibility for finances and lawsuits.

Limited Partnership: This structure is used for larger companies who have silent partners. Limited Partnership works similar to a General Partnership with the managing partners maintaining responsibility and liabilities of the company. Limited partners of the company are liable only for capital placed into the company. They have no authority in day-to-day operations. They are entitled to receive dividends and payouts from the company. Many family businesses use this structure to include their dependents in the profits without giving them any managing authority.

Limited Liability Company: This structure is the most used designation in small businesses. This structure protects all assets of the individuals who own the company. In most cases, it also protects the employees and the company itself. This means that if a lawsuit is filed against the Limited Liability Company, the owners and employees are not held personally responsible. Likewise, if a lawsuit is filed against a stakeholder, the company cannot be held liable. This company type has many tax advantages, too. Although there are single-member Limited Liability Companies, there are additional legal and tax advantages if the company has at least two members, regardless of distribution of shares. Limited Liability Companies enjoy taxation at a personal tax level instead of a higher corporate tax rate.

Corporation: A Corporation is separate from the members in every way. It is a separate entity for taxes and requires a separate corporate tax return. A Corporation is taxed on its profits at the end of the tax year. Corporations have evolved over many years and there is extensive case law. This makes it easier to know how a lawsuit will be handled should one arise. The main drawback of a Corporation is the amount of paperwork required to run under corporate laws. Most small businesses do not have the resources to comply with these laws and opt for the easier Limited Liability Company format. However, Corporations are far easier to take public and to sell on the stock market than the Limited Liability Companies.

S Corporation: The S Corporation is a hybrid of the Corporation and Partnership. The S Corporation offers all the benefits of a Corporation but allows pass through tax filing on personal returns like a Partnership. Extensive paperwork is still required with this structure.

Choosing the appropriate structure for your business is a major decision that requires intensive legal and financial consultations. Once you have chosen the best structure, the next thing you need to consider is whether you are going to have an open or closed business. The next chapter looks into this matter.

Chapter 2: Deciding Between an Open or Closed Company

Most first time entrepreneurs start an open company. They use the standard company templates found on various websites to outline business operations. This can be done with little to no investment up front. While this is an affordable choice, it may not be the best option.

As frequently happens in many companies, you may find one of your partners quitting after only a short time. That partner may find a buyer and sell out his shares without notifying you. If that person controls the company, then you may find the company turned into something very different from what you envisioned it to be. A closed company structure does not allow this to happen.

Standard templates do not use closed company language. If you are investing in your creative vision with a partner, you may need additional safeguards to protect the direction of the company. A closed company system will protect your investment in the venture. In a closed company, the selling partner offers the shares back to the company first. If the company cannot or does not want to buy the shares, the partner can then look for an outside buyer. However, the outside buyer has to be approved by the original partners. This gives the original partners the opportunity to assess if the third party will be a good fit for the company.

The downside to this may be the eventual liquidation of the company if a third party buyer could not be found. If the partner wants out, he may have to force the company to close in order to receive his investment back. This can lead to a difficult and long court process without guaranteed results. Just as you would with any other contract, carefully understand the clauses in a closed company Operating Agreement (OA). If there are parts that make you uncomfortable, do not move forward.

Most closed companies need unanimous agreement to change company direction. If a buyer is agreed upon, the new partner may not change the direction of the company even if he gets the majority shares. The inability to sell shares to anyone protects the company structure and mission. This is called being privately held. It means shares cannot be sold on an open market. This is especially important for family-run businesses. These safeguards make sure that a family name and vision remains intact in the face of an increasingly corporate environment.

After choosing the best structure and deciding on whether to make your company open or closed, you will need to put a detailed OA into writing. The rest of this book will focus on important items to include in the OA.

Chapter 3: Aligning Visions and Goals

Before writing the OA, many will begin with a letter of intent. This will outline each partner's point of view and expectations for the business. These letters can then be used by your lawyer as guidelines for the OA.

So what should be included in a letter of intent? First, write down what the business does. Understand each other's point of view and expectations for the business. Communicate what roles you will fill in the company. Also, state the roles you are not willing to fill. Be specific. If you are not willing to help with the accounting but do not mind scrubbing the occasional toilet, make sure you tell your partner. Neither of you can fill all the positions in the company. Be clear about what you can do. It will help you find the right employees for the jobs you cannot do.

You will also need to address basic operations. It may be best to create and fill out a questionnaire. Some questions to include are:

1. Will you be working on another job while starting this business?
2. If so, how much time can you give to the start-up?
3. List the days and hours you are available.
4. Do you expect to leave your current job to work full time at the start-up?
5. Do you have finances to be self-supporting until the start-up can afford to pay a salary?
6. What type of salary do you expect to earn from the start-up?

If one or both of you have another job, let each other know if you expect the business to match your current income so that you can come to the partnership full time. Be specific about the period when you want to see this happen. If both of you are clear with your goals for the partnership future disputes can be prevented. Also, be clear if you never intend the partnership to be a full time endeavor. Do not leave room for misunderstandings. If your intentions towards the business change over time, be upfront with that information, too. The more transparent you are in the early stages, the easier it will be to handle future discussions.

Once you have the letters of intent, take time to look at them separately. Consider if your expectations for the business align with those of your partner. If they do, then you are ready to write the OA. If they do not, then you need to talk about the letter together. Consider taking a few days in a neutral place to discuss how you and your partner can move forward with the business despite conflicting expectations. See if you can agree on the purpose of the business. This period is critical in your pending endeavor with your partner. When working out details, are you able to come to fair solutions? Are you able to talk or has the time been spent arguing? These are indicators as to whether the partnership will work or will cause you a lot of discomfort and loss.

Once you are confident that you and your new partner are a good match, it is time to define each person's roles and responsibilities. This is covered in the next chapter.

Chapter 4: Defining Roles and Responsibilities

One person cannot fulfill all the roles in a company. Even Sole Proprietors and single-member Limited Liability Companies hire contractors and employees to fill positions the owner cannot do. Most companies hire tax consultants, certified public accountants, bookkeepers, and lawyers to do the legal side of the business. Hiring for other positions should be treated with the same level of importance.

For example, an architect earns $250 an hour drafting plans for housing developments. The architect is capable and enjoys cleaning the office, a $10 an hour position. Does it make sense for the architect to spend that hour cleaning to save $10 for the business since cleaning is something enjoyable? The answer is a resounding no! That is a $240 an hour loss. It is more sensible for the architect to spend that hour working on drafting plans and hire another person to do the cleaning.

The same thought process needs to be used when deciding roles and responsibilities with your partner. Be clear what each person's roles are and stick with it. Do not be afraid to hire a third party to do the work that neither partner likes to do. If one is good at design and another at bookkeeping, but neither wants to pick up the phone, then hire a receptionist. Be clear about your likes and dislikes as well as strengths and weaknesses.

Set clear guidelines about available time to work on the business. Be realistic and up front with your needs. If one of you has another job, then that person cannot be expected to be at meetings or functions during his work hours in his other job. As long as these issues are addressed up front, then there should be no problems in the long run. Be specific and put everything into black and white. At the same time, be flexible as schedules change.

While deciding roles, work out who will be the boss and who will be the spokesperson of the company. Each of you may want power roles so you need to set what power each of you may have. Perhaps one oversees employees while the other manages contracts or public engagements. These are things needed to be decided on early in the relationship. Outline each person's duties and responsibilities in the OA along with the official titles used. For example, you may be the Chief Executive Officer (CEO) while your partner may be the Chief Financial Officer (CFO).

Also, decide if a partner wants to be designated silent, meaning investing money but not taking a working role in the company. A silent partner does not vote on company matters either. More often than not, the public does not even know who the silent partner is. Silent partners are a great way to bring an infusion of cash without the added stress of another person co-managing the business.

Once roles and responsibilities are determined, make sure each person is doing their job. There should be a system in place to monitor the work expected from each partner. Good intentions are still just intentions. There has to be an incentive for work done. This is very important in the start-up phase of a business. It is easy to get caught up in life and produce only excuses why the work is not done.

Consider using financial incentives, a system of debits and credits for set job duties. When starting a business it is hard to log all the hours put into the start-up phase. Many sleepless nights are spent calculating costs and researching products. It is easy to get side tracked on things you like to research versus the tasks that need to be completed. Have a weekly meeting to set realistic goals for the work expected. Then place an incentive upon completing those goals. It could be as simple as a pizza at the end of the week or placing a $5 bill in the petty cash for uncompleted items. This will help keep you motivated when a paycheck is not a reality yet.

Money is a key motivator in any business. It is crucial to address the financial side of partnerships in writing. The next chapter will look at how to split the expenses and profits of a business with your partner.

Chapter 5: Establishing How to Split Expenses and Profits

How to split expenses and profits can be a complicated matter. It is best to set this up based upon the recommendations of your lawyer and accountant before starting business. This chapter will review a few examples of what can be done.

Decide at the beginning how much cash you can contribute to the business. Estimate if there will be additional funds available for business expenses. Be clear how much of your liquidity be invested in the partnership. Do not go past this cash value and do not put your family finances at risk. Labor is just as valuable as cash in a start-up.

If both partners are bringing cash to the start-up of equal value and both partners will spend equal amounts of time on the business, then consider splitting ownership 50/50. By splitting the ownership 50/50, both partners will get an equal share of the profits at the end of the year after expenses are paid. Both partners are entitled to a salary and profit distribution. This is the most straightforward partnership possible.

The partnership can be structured differently if the cash contribution is not equal. If Partner A brings $25,000 and Partner B brings $75,000, then the structure could be 25/75. However, the partners can agree to keep a 50/50 ownership with a different dividend payout until Partner B is paid back $50,000. When $50,000 is paid back to Partner B, then the dividend payout reverts to a 50/50 format.

Things get a little more complicated when one partner brings cash and the other brings labor or professional experience. Partner A brings $25,000 cash and no experience whereas Partner B brings an established client list and experience in the industry. At this point Partner B's experience may be more valuable than the cash contribution of Partner A. The partners may agree to a 40/60 ownership model.

All these models change if only one partner will be active in the day-to-day business. As you can see, this can get complicated quickly. Just like everything else in a partnership start-up, meet with the professionals. During the negotiation process, both you and your partner should have separate lawyers. This is to keep fresh eyes and a different perspective on the contractual agreements.

Money can be the end of a good partnership. If your business makes large profits, make sure those profits are protected. Protecting yourself when banking with a partner is addressed in the next chapter.

Chapter 6: Protecting Yourself When Banking with a Partner

When collaborating on an OA, be specific with all banking clauses. Your bank can only protect you if you put in specific statements within the OA. Things to consider adding to the OA:

1. State who can open bank accounts and what type of accounts are allowed by the company. State if business credit cards, debits cards, and checks will be used. If you allow these tools to be used by employees, make sure there are daily spending limits on each card and dual signatures required on large checks. Then, set up mobile banking alerts so you can keep tabs on what is being spent. These simple monitoring tools will help catch any misuse of company funds quickly.

2. Decide who has the power to sign checks. For added protection, require two signatures on any check over $1000.

3. State who can wire transfer funds out of the accounts and how much. Again, it is advisable

to require a secondary voice authentication other than the authorized originating member. These are safeguards that will cut out the ability to move large withdrawals out of the account without both partners being aware. You have worked hard to earn the money. Make sure it stays in your business until you agree to move the money.

4. State that both partners must be present to close the account if the account is over $1000. If one cannot be present, require a notarized statement of agreement to close the account and how the funds are to be distributed.

5. Determine if business loans are allowed and who can sign for one.

These clauses are not all inclusive. Your lawyer will suggest more safeguards. The main point to keep in mind is to know who has access to the company funds and how much liability each person holds. Your lawyer may even suggest individual liability contracts be signed by every person who has access to the business funds.

A note on business loans and credit cards: Whenever you open an account for your business, make sure you sign in your legal capacity as a member of the business. If possible, never give a personal guarantee for credit. The point of having a Limited Liability Company or Corporation is to cut out personal liability. Your signature is very important when signing any contracts for the business. Your legal signature is covered in the next chapter.

Chapter 7: Signing Your Legal Signature

Many people do not realize that a signature binds an entrepreneur to a contract personally if not signed properly. If you sign a contract for your business but do not include your title in the business, then you have just guaranteed the contract. You will not be reminded to sign in the capacity of a business owner or authorized agent. It is your responsibility to know and remember to do this.

When signing a document of any type for your business, write your name then a comma followed by your title. Make sure the company name is located directly below and is written out in full. An example is shown below.

Mya N. Reed, Manager

Reed Contracts Limited Liability Company,

A Wyoming Closed Company.

Along with signing the document at the end, pay close attention to how you are listed in the body of the document. If you are signing the contract as an authorized agent of the company, make sure this is reflected in the document. Any typo in the document, such as your name without reference to your title or your company, will legally bind you to the contract. If your company cannot make the payments, you will be required to do so.

Review all contracts with the help of a trusted lawyer. Make sure all parties of the contract have been listed properly with titles. Do not sign unless it is clear that you do not have personal liability for the contract. Also, verify that every person listed on the contract is authorized by his respective company/companies to enter into the contract.

These are good guidelines to follow for all documents within your partnership as well. The next chapter lists several agreements that should be signed by both partners before starting business.

Chapter 8: Partnership Agreements to Put in Writing

This book has touched on several areas that should be well thought of and put in writing before starting a partnership. This chapter lists a few more areas to consider.

1. Decision Making Authority: In the day-to-day operations, it is almost impossible to run every decision past your partner. There needs to be a defined list of decision-making responsibilities that each partner can make without written approval from the other partner. Think in terms of daily operations. What is necessary and normal during the day?

2. Salaries and Distributions: This was touched on in Chapter 5 but warrants another mention. Be clear with each other on these points. Negotiate suitable salaries up front. Decide if year-end profits will stay in the company for a certain number of years or if distributions will be paid. Discuss terms for bonuses and increases in salary. Put it all in writing and sign the agreement in your legal capacity.

3. <u>Vacation and Sick Leave:</u> It is important to decide up front if vacation or sick leave will be paid. Set the time available for such leave. Also, make terms for more vacation and sick leave based on years and seniority in the company.

4. <u>Health Care and Other Benefits:</u> Decide if the company will give benefits or supplement the costs of benefits for the partners and employees. Make provisions for changing all contracts later based on needs of the company.

5. <u>Disagreement Resolution:</u> A disagreement may come up that may not be easily resolved. Make provisions now for arbitration and court actions while you are amicable. Decide where arbitration should take place and who handles the expenses incurred. Do this for any potential court case as well. Do not take this for granted. In a mobile society, it is important to set the place up front. That way if one partner moves away, that partner cannot expect the other to answer a court hearing in a different jurisdiction. Make it clear now.

Disagreement resolution is not something people like to think about going into a new partnership. The reality is disagreements happen. They can destroy a partnership if not handled properly. This is why it is important to have an exit strategy should the need arise. The last chapter will address the exit strategy, how to dissolve a partnership.

Chapter 9: Dissolving the Partnership

One of the first things to do when drafting the OA is to decide how the company will be handled if it is dissolved or if one person wants out of the partnership. This was touched on in the Chapter 2; *Should You have an Open or Closed Company?* However, it is so important we will look at the exit strategy again. When one partner wants to get out of the business altogether, then he needs to set a price at which the other partner can buy the shares. If the other partner cannot or does not want to buy them, then a third party can be found.

Should a third party not be found and the partner will not buy the remaining shares, there should be a clause for liquidating the company. This is when the entire company will be sold and both partners paid out according to the OA. If the company is not purchased by a third party, then the company will close and all assets liquidated.

All assets should have been assigned a value at time of purchase or at tax time by your accountant. The assets can be sold and profits distributed according to the OA after all expenses are paid. Alternatively, if both parties agree, physical assets can be distributed to the partners after all debts are paid. It will be each partner's responsibility to meet with a tax professional about any capital gains or other taxes incurred upon distribution of assets and funds from a dissolved company.

Provisions for dissolving a partnership can be simple or complex depending on the structure of the business, capital contributions, and outstanding contracts among other factors. Consult with your attorney in the start-up phase to make sure both partners will be treated fairly if the need to dissolve the company arises.

Conclusion

Creating business partnerships is exciting. Often overwhelmed by excitement, new entrepreneurs go into business without defining the most basic functions of the company. There are many issues to consider and to resolve in order to protect yourself and your business. Begin your partnership with clear communication. Put everything in writing, so there won't be misunderstandings later.

Create a legally binding OA to define each partner's role, responsibilities, authority, liability, and payout. During the process of creating this contract, you will get a feel for your compatibility. Did you collaborate or argue? Is this partnership viable based on these interactions? If there are any doubts do not move forward. It is better to find a different partner than set yourself up for trouble later.

Learn to look at all documents with your attorney. It may seem costly to do this, but it will save you vast amounts of money and energy later should you need to litigate for breach of contract. Using separate attorneys will also help to keep all contracts fair. Each attorney should negotiate the best options for each client and help to compromise on areas of disagreement.

There are many areas to consider when starting a partnership. This book is a good place to start and should help you open a dialogue with your potential partner and lawyer. It cannot be stressed enough that clear communication in a written format is the rule of successful partnerships. Well-written contracts will make starting and ending a partnership easier for both parties. This foresight may also help to keep your relationship the same as it was before starting the business together.

Finally, I'd like to thank you for purchasing this book! If you enjoyed it or found it helpful, I'd greatly appreciate it if you'd take a moment to leave a review on Amazon. Thank you!

Made in the USA
Monee, IL
30 August 2020